Baking with Knox the Knight

By Eliza Webb

Queen Carmen stood in front of her knights.

She planned to throw herself a birthday party and needed some yummy food to serve.

“Comb the land for the best dish,” said the Queen.
“The winning knight will sit with me at my birthday feast.”

Knox knew just who to see.

He climbed on his horse, Malcolm, and raced to the far side of Knob Hill.

Dora the baker lived deep in the woods.
Her small cabin was draped in gnarly, knotty vines.

Knox knocked.

Dora stopped knitting.

“Who could that be?” she thought.

"Hi, Knox!" said Dora.
"What's up?"

"Dora, do you know a dish good enough for the Queen's birthday party?" Knox asked.
"I have never baked a thing before!"

He went inside the cosy cabin.

"The Queen **loves** my salt bread!" said Dora.
"She always asks for it."

"Please can you teach me how to make it?" asked Knox.
"I don't want to get it wrong."

“Be calm, Knox,” said Dora.
“We’ll bake it together!
These days, all knights should
know how to bake.”

Dora showed Knox what he would need to make the salt bread mix.

Knox stirred the mix together. Then, he rubbed a knob of butter into the mix with his fingers and thumbs.

Then Knox kneaded the mix with his knuckles and palms.
He kneaded the mix until it became stretchy.

With a knife, Dora cut the mix into strands and knotted them together.

Back at the palace, Queen Carmen gnawed on the knights' dishes.

She tried each dish.

The best dish is the salt bread made by Knox!

Knox's legs went numb with shock, and he fell to his knees.

He had made the winning dish!

CHECKING FOR MEANING

1. What was the name of Knox's horse? *(Literal)*
2. What did Dora stop doing when Knox arrived at her cabin? *(Literal)*
3. Was Knox good at making salt bread? How do you know? *(Inferential)*
4. How would you feel if you were asked to make a dish for a queen? *(Evaluative)*

EXTENDING VOCABULARY

draped	Dora's cabin was *draped in gnarly, knotty vines*. What does it mean if the vines are draped? What is another word with a similar meaning?
knotty	Which letter in the word *knotty* is silent? The vines on Dora's cabin were knotty. What does that mean? What else can get knotty?
numb	Which letter in the word *numb* is silent? What does it feel like if your legs go numb?

MOVING BEYOND THE TEXT

1. What special food would you request for a celebration?
2. What types of food might people bring to a celebration?
3. Dora was an expert in baking. Are you an expert in anything? What would you like to become an expert in?
4. Have you ever had to ask someone for help to achieve a goal? What happened?

TIME TO WRITE

Imagine you are going to a party. Write about something special you would make or bake for the celebration.